Flag Down!

by Deborah Nash
Illustrated by Bill Ledger

OXFORD
UNIVERSITY PRESS

Tricky words to practise before reading this book:

story, were, come, said, there, like, out

Jin

Jin can zoom up and up. He can go as high as a rocket.

Magnus
(caretaker)

Jin and Magnus were in the garden.
"The flag has come down," Jin said.

"Wait there, Jin," said Magnus. "I will get a ladder from my shed."

"We will not need a ladder," Jin said to himself. "I can put the flag back up."

Jin shot up in the air with the flag.

A gust of wind hit Jin.
He had to drop the flag.

The flag floated off.
Jin went to grab it.

The wind swept the flag up. Jin was going too fast to stop.
Jin got twisted up in the flag.

Jin started to spin down.
"This was not part of the plan!" he said.

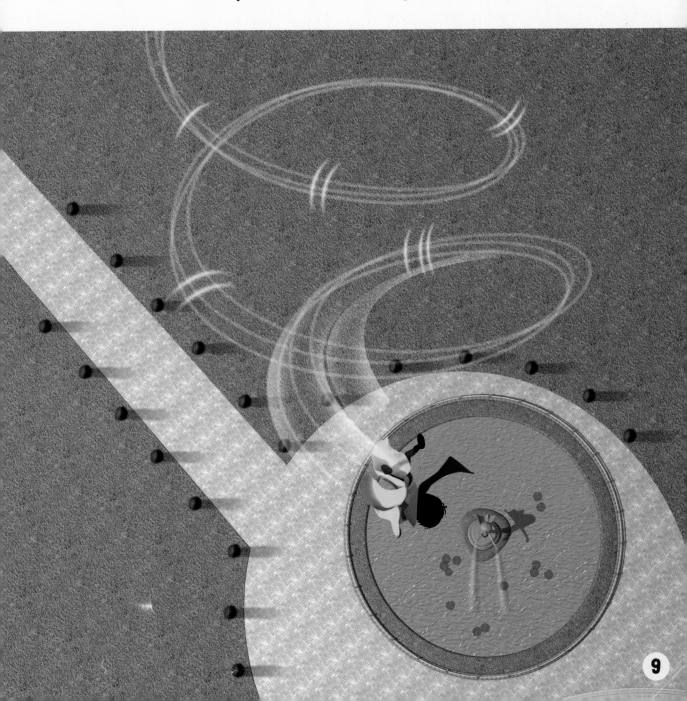

Jin landed in the pond. It was not deep.

Jin was glad to be down again.

"I did not like that," he said.

Jin got some pondweed out of his hair.

"Jin, I said to wait!" Magnus said. "Now the flag is dripping wet."

"I am wet too," said Jin, with a frown.

"I will put the flag up," said Magnus.
"I will help you," Jin said.

"Thanks," Magnus said, "but you will need
to put that frog back!"

Retell the story ...

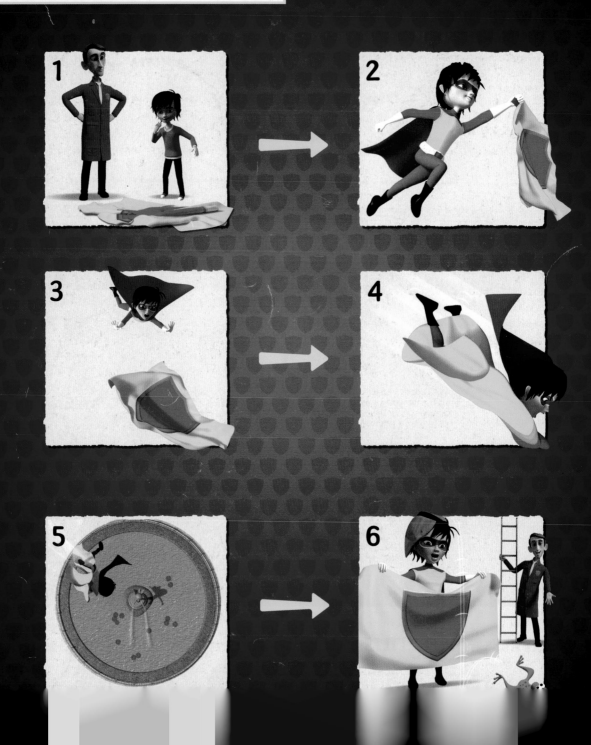